# CONTENTS

All words in **bold** can be found in the glossary on page 31.

# A WORLD FULL OF CARS

Cars are a huge and important part of our lives. We travel in them – to the shops, to school or on holiday. We build millions of kilometres of roads for them, through cities and across the countryside, all over the world. We spend vast amounts of money buying, fuelling and maintaining them.

# BIGGER AND FASTER

The first petrol-driven cars took to the roads in the 1880s. They were noisy and hard to control. They were also very slow, with a top speed of about 9 mph (15 kph). Modern cars are quieter, easier to drive, and can go at high speeds – although the legal speed limit in most countries is between 70 and 80 mph (112 and 130 kph).

## CAR JOKE

**Q** When is a car not a car?

**A** When it turns into a road!

Some cars are very big. The biggest sports utility vehicles (SUVs) [above], are as large and powerful as a light truck. Other cars are very small. The tiny Smart Car (left) has just two seats, and is so short it is easy to park. But most cars are somewhere in the middle.

# THE MAIN PARTS OF A CAR

- The body is the outer casing. It is made of steel, plastic or **fibreglass**.
- The chassis is the frame. The body and other parts are fixed to this.
- The wheels have rubber tyres filled with air.
- The engine provides the power.

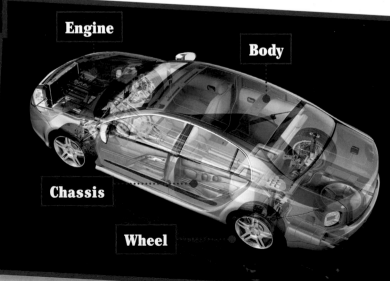

Engine

Body

Chassis

Wheel

# DRIVING FORCE

The most common type of car engine is called an internal combustion (burning inside) engine. A mixture of fuel and air is fed into a **cylinder** called a combustion chamber (below, 1) and **compressed** (2). Here it is lit by a spark and explodes. The explosion heats the air inside the cylinder and makes it expand. This pushes down a rod called a piston (3). As the air cools, the piston returns to the top of the cylinder and pushes the gases back out (4).

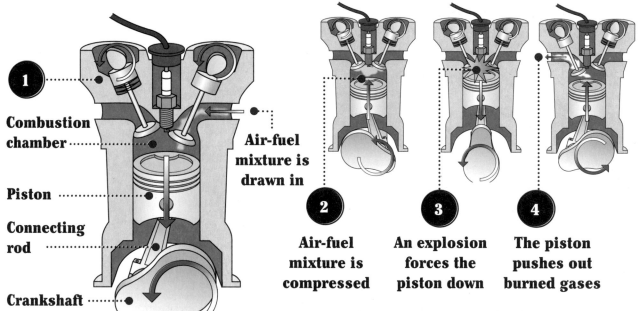

**1**

Combustion chamber

Air-fuel mixture is drawn in

Piston

Connecting rod

Crankshaft

**2**

Air-fuel mixture is compressed

**3**

An explosion forces the piston down

**4**

The piston pushes out burned gases

# TURNING THE WHEELS

How does the motion of the pistons make the wheels move? The up-and-down motion is converted into a round-and-round motion by the **crankshaft**. From here the force is passed on to the **axle**, which is joined to the wheels. In most cars, the engine's power turns only the two front wheels. This is called a two-wheel drive system.

A mechanic removes the axle from the car he is repairing.

Cars giving off fumes.

**Exhaust pipe**

# ENERGY FOR ENGINES

Fuels made from **petroleum**, such as petrol and diesel, are used in most cars. But there are two big problems with petroleum. We are using so much of it that supplies could run out in the future. Petrol engines also give off **exhaust** fumes, which go out through a tube (above) called the exhaust pipe. These waste gases are damaging the environment.

Scientists are developing engines that use other kinds of energy. Some modern cars are powered by electricity stored in batteries. Others burn natural gas, and others use biofuel (a chemical made from vegetable crops). Some even use the power of the Sun's rays. This is called solar power.

## AMAZING FACT
## Chip shop power

Cars can run on old cooking oil. Some have specially converted engines that burn used vegetable oil from chip shops and other fast-food outlets. They work well but they smell like food cooking when they drive along!

Panels on a solar car change the energy in sunlight into electricity.

# POWER TO THE WHEELS

## INTO GEAR

Do you ride a bike with gears? It's harder going uphill, so you change into a lower gear. This helps you put more power into the bike. A car's gearbox works in the same way. The engine needs more power to go uphill, and less to go downhill. The driver can change gear to keep the car travelling as smoothly and **efficiently** as possible.

## AMAZING FACT
### Horsepower

We measure the force of an engine in units called 'horsepower'. This is because early inventors compared their engines to the power of a horse. An engine with the same strength as one horse is a 1 hp (horsepower) engine. One of the most powerful cars for sale today is the HTT Pléthore. Its 1,300-horsepower engine gives the car the same power-to-weight ratio as a Formula 1 car.

The chassis and body of the HTT Pléthore is made entirely out of carbon fibre. Carbon fibre is an extremely strong and light material, in which several thousand fibres of carbon are bonded together in crystals.

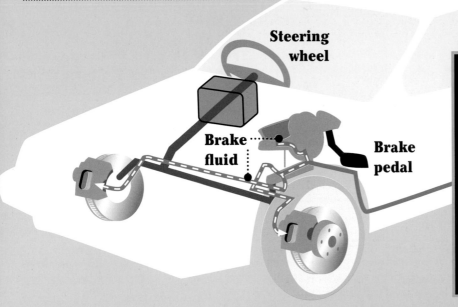

**Steering wheel**

**Brake fluid**

**Brake pedal**

## TRUE OR FALSE?

The driver of a car travelling at 70 mph (113 kph) uses up the length of a tennis court to bring the car to an emergency stop. **True or False?**

**FALSE! The stopping distance of a car going at 70 mph (113 kph) is 96 metres, the length of four tennis courts!**

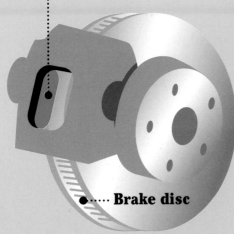

**Brake pad**

**Brake disc**

# STEERING AND STOPPING

Other parts of the car are just as important as the engine. Imagine having no brakes and no steering wheel! The steering wheel controls the direction the car is travelling in. The driver turns it, and the car's front wheels turn in the same direction.

The brakes make the car slow down or stop. Each wheel has a brake disc attached to it. When the driver presses on the brake pedal, liquid is pushed down a tube. This forces the brake pads to clamp onto the discs and slows them down to a stop.

## AMAZING FACT
### Death on the roads

Driving can be very dangerous. Well over one million people are killed in road accidents every year throughout the world. More than 50 million are injured.

# SPORTS CARS

Sports cars are built to be quick and fun to drive. Most sports cars have seats for only two people. Many are convertibles, meaning they have roofs which can be opened or removed to let in light and air. Above all, these cars can speed up very quickly, and are light and easy to handle.

Mazda MX-5

L·EV·MX 521

# WHAT MAKES A SPORTS CAR SPORTY?

Many features help sports cars to go fast. They have powerful engines and lightweight bodies. The bodies have a **streamlined** shape, which means they cut through the air faster with less **wind resistance**. They are also low to the ground, so they are less likely to flip over or skid at high speeds.

## TRUE OR FALSE?

The man who invented the famous Lamborghini sports car started off building farm tractors. **True or False?**

**TRUE!** Ferruccio Lamborghini had a tractor factory before he became interested in sports cars.

The Gallardo (above) is the most popular model of Lamborghini. Over 14,000 have been built since 2003.

# SPRINGS AND SUSPENSION

All car wheels have springs, which soften the shocks from bumps in the road. This is the **suspension** system. Each wheel has its own set of springs so that it can move up and down independently (on its own). This helps the car to grip the road better. To stop the springs being too bouncy a car uses **hydraulic** shock absorbers. A piston inside the shock absorber is connected to the spring. When the car hits a bump a tube in the shock absorber fills with oil, which slows down the piston and in turn slows down the spring.

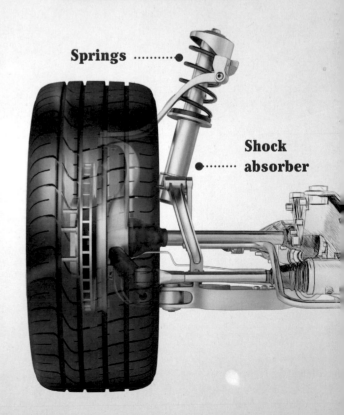

Springs

Shock absorber

# SUPERCARS

Supercars are for people who want to be looked at – and have lots of money. They are the fastest and most expensive cars on the road. They have huge and powerful engines, and are easy to drive at speed. Most supercars also look unusual and eye-catching.

Above all, supercars are rare and special. They are so expensive that few people can afford them. Many are produced in limited editions, so very few are for sale. Some are specially **adapted** versions of ordinary cars, with dramatic bodywork and engines capable of massive **acceleration** and speed.

## TRUE OR FALSE?

The Rolls Royce is the original supercar. The city which boasts the most Rolls Royce cars is London. **True or False?**

**FALSE!** Hong Kong in China has the most Rolls Royces – an amazing 1,500!

## FAMOUS SUPERCARS

One of the very first supercars was the Bentley Speed Six of 1928. It was not only very expensive, it also won many early motor races. Only 182 Speed Sixes were ever made, and they are rare and treasured items today.

The SSC Tuatara is a new supercar manufactured by Shelby SuperCars. It is expected to achieve a whopping top speed of 276 mph (444 kph) making it the fastest road car in the world.

# RACING DRIVER FOR A DAY

Visitors to the Nurburgring motorsport complex in Germany can test their motor-racing skills. They can drive their own vehicles around the old Northern Loop, once used for Formula One (F1) races. There is no speed limit and the circuit is one way, so they can drive as fast as they like.

## AMAGING FACT
### The most expensive car

The world's most expensive new car is the Bugatti Veyron Super Sports. You could buy one if you had a spare £1.5 million (2.4 million dollars). The Veyron accelerates faster than any other legal road car, going from 0 to 60 mph (97 kph) in just 2.5 seconds!

# RACING CARS

A racing car is specially built to take part in races. It doesn't carry luggage or passengers. It has a simple aim – to go as fast as possible over a set distance. Races take place on circuits or roads, so cars are designed and built to go around bends and other hazards really fast.

Car racing began not long after petrol-engined cars were invented. The very first organised race took place between Paris and Rouen in France, in 1894. Twenty-five competitors started the 79-mile (127-km) race. The winner crossed the line in just under seven hours at an average speed of less than 12 mph (19 kph)!

## FORMULA ONE

A Formula One (F1) car has a single seat and a powerful engine which takes it to speeds of 200 mph (320 kph). It also has **aerodynamic** fittings called 'wings' at the front and rear. These channel the wind to create a **downforce**, which pushes the car downwards. This makes the car more stable when it is tearing around bends.

## AMAZING FACT
### The greatest?

The most successful of all Formula One racing drivers is Michael Schumacher who retired in 2012. He holds the record for the most championship wins, race victories, fastest laps and **pole positions**. In 2004 Schumacher finished the season with a record 148 points and set a new record of 13 race wins out of a possible 18.

## SCHUMACHER - THE STATS!

Championships – 7

Race wins – 91

Fastest laps – 77

Pole positions – 68

# TOURING RACE CARS

Touring cars (right) are ordinary makes of car, modified to take part in circuit races. These racers have special brakes, suspension, wheels and engines, as well as aerodynamic wings.

# RALLY CARS

Rally cars race along narrow country tracks or roads closed to other traffic. Some rallies cross ice, deserts or mountains. Rally cars are beefed-up versions of standard saloon cars. A navigator sits beside the driver to warn him or her of hazards and make sure they take the correct route.

## AMAZING FACT
### Nine in a row!

Frenchman Sébastien Loeb is a rallying superstar. He has won the World Championship an incredible nine times running between 2004 and 2012. During his career he has racked up a massive 900 stage wins!

Rally drivers deliberately slide the car sideways to get around tight bends quickly.

Custom cars are decorated to make them stand out from the crowd.

**CAR JOKE**

**Q** What do you call someone with a car on his head?

**A** Jack!

# CUSTOM CARS

Fresh from the factory, all car models look the same. However, some drivers like to make their cars look different. They change the body shape, the engine and the wheels. They add decorations, and paint fantastic colours and designs. This is called 'customising' a car.

Most custom car fanatics start with the engine. They replace the standard engine with something much more powerful, such as a Chevrolet V-8 (left). Bigger wheels are fitted with wider tyres for better grip.

Customisers can improve old cars by giving them bigger wheels and powerful engines.

The car body gets even more work. The customiser cuts away parts of the sheet metal, to make it look lower or more streamlined. Then the pieces are **welded** together again. Metal fins can be added, as well as big bumpers, **radiator grilles** and shiny metal side strips.

## PAINT JOB

Custom car bodies are painted in bright and unusual colours. Some are yellow, some red, some purple. Many coats are needed to build up a deep and shiny effect. On top of this go pictures or other designs. The most popular designs are flames, spreading from front to back.

### AMAZING FACT
### Marvellous Merc

The Hirohata Merc (above) is the most famous custom car of all time. It appeared in many magazines and its style has been a huge inspiration to custom car builders ever since. Built in 1953, it began as a standard car. The body was given a new and smoother shape. Many new parts were added, including grilles, giant chrome bumpers and spotlights. The car was finished with 30 coats of paint!

# OFF-ROAD CARS

Off-road cars are specially made to drive on surfaces other than roads. In spite of the name, they can easily drive on roads as well. But, unlike ordinary cars, they can deal with rough tracks, muddy fields, sandy deserts and even steep mountainsides.

The first ORVs (off-road vehicles) were built for farmers, foresters and other people who had to drive in difficult terrain. They included two world-famous makes, the Land Rover and the Jeep. Both of these, launched in the 1940s, are still widely used.

## AMAZING FACT
### Best in the Desert

The Best in the Desert (BITD) racing association organises off-road races in the American deserts. There are events for all kinds of ORVs from **dune buggies** and quad bikes, to cars and trucks. Desert races are long and in remote terrain. They test the endurance of the driver and machine. The Vegas to Reno race is the longest off-road race in the US covering a distance up to a 1,000 miles (1,600 km)!

An off-road car makes short work of a muddy obstacle.

# OFF-ROAD SPORTS

Today, ORVs are very popular for leisure and for sport. Sporting events include rallies and desert racing. Rock crawling (right) is a race over very rough ground, with boulders, rock piles and other obstacles. Rock crawling drivers have to go very slowly and carefully.

# WHAT MAKES THEM DIFFERENT?

Off-road vehicles have big wheels to keep them high off the ground. Wide tyres stop them sinking into soft ground, mud or sand. The deep grooves and large bumps on the tyres help the vehicle grip on slippery surfaces. Extra low gears help them to move slowly through boggy and steep terrain. Most important of all, they have a **four-wheel drive** system, which delivers power to each of the wheels at the same time. Most ordinary cars only have two-wheel drive systems.

## TRUE OR FALSE?

The actor Arnold Schwarzenegger inspired the launch of the giant 'Hummer' SUV. **True or False?**

**TRUE!** The Hummer was originally just a military vehicle. A version for everyday use went on sale after a campaign by the film star in 1992.

# MILITARY CARS

Cars are a vital part of today's armed forces. But they are very different from the cars you see on the street. Most military cars are covered in armour to protect them from shells and bombs, and carry guns for attacking the enemy. They are used for many important jobs, such as gathering information and controlling crowds.

## AMAZING FACT
### The first armoured car

One of the first armoured military vehicles was the Motor War Car, built in Britain in 1902. It had a skirt of armour which looked like an upside down bath. The Motor War Car carried two machine guns and had a top speed of 9 mph (14 kph). However, It could not travel over rough ground and was never actually used in warfare.

This huge military car is carrying a missile system for shooting down enemy aircraft.

## MILITARY CAR JOKE

Knock! Knock!
Who's there?
Tank!
Tank who?
You're welcome!

# FROM SMALL...

The British Ferret (right) was a famous light-armoured car. It had four wheels, and was armed with a machine gun and six grenade launchers. Too small for heavy fighting, the Ferret was fast and nimble enough to be used in city streets and other confined spaces.

## ...TO BIG!

The US Army's M1128 Mobile Gun System (MGS) looks like a tank. It has eight big wheels and is nearly as long as a bus! The MGS has a crew of three. Its big gun is mounted in a **turret**, which can rotate. It fires up to six shells per minute.

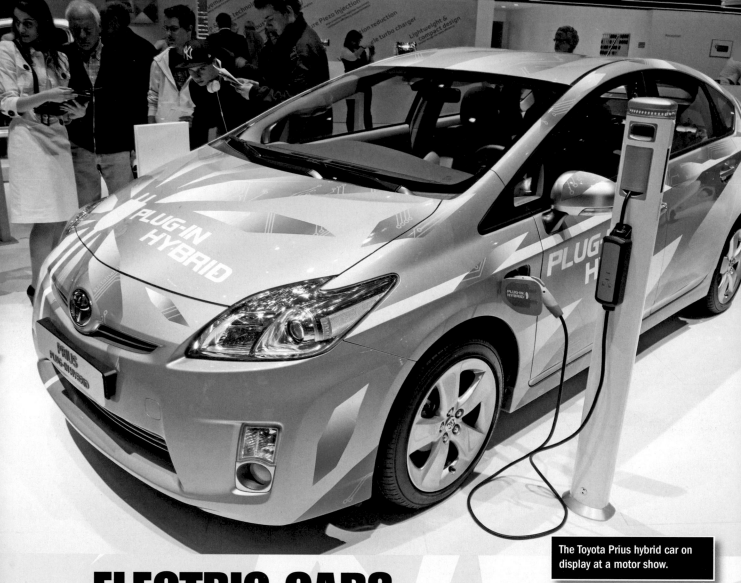

The Toyota Prius hybrid car on display at a motor show.

# ELECTRIC CARS

An electric car is powered by an electric motor instead of a petrol engine. The motor uses energy from a battery, which stores electricity. The battery can be recharged by simply plugging it into the household power supply. On one charge, the electric car can travel about 100 miles (160km).

Hybrid cars run on both petrol and electricity. In some hybrids, the petrol engine and an electric motor work together to power the car. Other vehicles such as the popular Toyota Prius are powered by an electric motor when they are moving slowly (up to around 15 mph [24 kph]) and switch to using a petrol engine when they reach a higher speed. Both types of hybrid use less fuel than ordinary petrol-engined cars.

## CAR JOKE

**Q** What happened to the frog when his car broke down?

**A** He got toad away!

## AMAGING FACT
# Electric best-seller

The world's best-selling electric car is the Nissan Leaf. Launched in Japan in 2010, it is a five-door family-sized car. The Leaf costs about $30,000 and more than 20,000 have been sold.

A row of Nissan Leafs are plugged in to have their batteries charged.

# ELECTRIC V PETROL

In many ways, electric cars win out over petrol-engined ones. Their motors are simple, with no complicated cylinders, pistons and fuel pipes. They do not release exhaust fumes, which cause a lot of harm to the environment. And they are cheaper to run – electricity costs less than petrol. But petrol cars are still much cheaper to buy, so most people drive them.

## TRUE OR FALSE?

An electric car once held the world speed record. **True or False?**

**TRUE!** In 1899, the rocket-shaped Jamais Contente reached a record speed of 65 mph (105 kph) near Paris. It had an electric engine.

The record-breaking Jamais Contente.

*Thrust SSC*

# THE FASTEST CARS

Ever since cars were invented, people have wanted them to go faster and faster. The present land speed record is 763 mph (1,228 kph). This is faster than the speed of sound! It was set in 1997 by the car *Thrust SSC*, powered by two giant **jet engines**.

Now a new car is being developed to beat that record. The *Bloodhound SSC* will have three engines – a jet engine, a rocket engine and a petrol engine used in F1 racing cars. It aims to travel at over 1,000 mph (1,600 kph).

*Bloodhound SSC*

# DRIVEN BY WHEELS

In many ways, jet vehicles are not cars at all. They are propelled along by the blast of air from their jet or rocket engines. Ordinary cars are propelled by engines that turn their wheels. The world speed record for a wheel-driven car is 458 mph (737 kph), set by the *Vesco Turbinator* in 2001.

## AMAZING FACT
### Top 10 landmarks in speed

|  |  |  |
|------|---------|-------|
| 1898 | French electric car | 39 mph (63 kph).. |
| 1906 | The US steam-powered *Rocket* | 126 mph (205 kph) |
| 1927 | US petrol-powered *Mystery* | 200 mph (320 kph) |
| 1939 | British *Railton Special* | 367 mph (588 kph) |
| 1964 | British *Bluebird* | 400 mph (640 kph) |
| 1965 | US *Spirit of America* | 600 mph (960 kph) |
| 1970 | US rocket-powered *Blue Flame* | 622 mph (1,001 kph) |
| 1983 | British turbojet *Thrust2* | 633 mph (1,019 kph) |
| 1987 | British *Thrust SSC* | 714 mph (1,149 kph) |
| 1997 | British *Thrust SSC* | 763 mph (1,228 kph) |

## TRUE OR FALSE?

Vehicles cannot travel on the Moon. **True or False?**

**FALSE!** In 1972 astronaut Eugene Cernan drove his Lunar Explorer at 10.5 mph (17 kph) – the fastest anyone has travelled on the Moon.

*Vesco Turbinator*

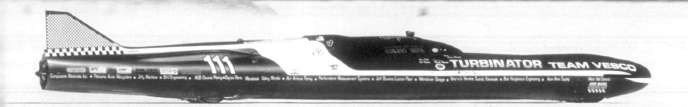

# QUIZ

How much have you learned from reading this book? Here is a quiz to test your memory.

1. In drag racing, what is a 'funny car'?

2. What do we call a car powered by both electricity and a petrol engine?

3. Which F1 driver has won the most Grand Prix races?

4. What do the initials ORV stand for?

5. What does 'internal combustion' mean?

6. Is a Smart Car very big or very small?

7. Which causes the most pollution – a petrol-driven car or an electric car?

8. In what year was the first organised car race?

9. How do you 'customise' a car?

10. Why do off-road cars have big wide tyres?

11. How many wheels does the M1128 Mobile Gun System have?

12. What do drag racers call their trial run?

13. What part of a car is the chassis?

14. Why are sports cars streamlined?

15. How many seats does an F1 racing car have?

# GLOSSARY

**accelerating** increasing speed

**adapted** made or changed for a special purpose

**aerodynamic** made with rounded or smooth edges and outlines, to reduce the wind resistance

**axle** the rod fixed to the centre of a wheel that turns the wheel

**crankshaft** the main shaft of an engine that carries the force from the pistons to the wheels

**compressed** squeezed into less space

**cylinder** the tube-shaped container in a car engine in which a piston slides up and down

**downforce** a force pressing a moving vehicle down towards the ground

**dune buggy** an open-topped vehicle specially made to drive on sand dunes and other rough or soft surfaces

**efficiently** with the minimum amount of effort or expense

**exhaust** the pipe through which the gases from burned fuel are released

**fibreglass** a plastic material with fibres of glass fixed in it to make it stronger

**four-wheel drive** a system where power is transmitted from the engine directly to all four wheels of a vehicle

**hydraulic** relating to power that comes from pushing liquid through a tight space

**jet engine** an engine sending out a high-powered stream of gas backwards, which drives a vehicle forwards

**petroleum** a naturally occurring oil that is processed to make fuels such as diesel and petrol (gasoline), among many other things

**pole position** the position at the front of the grid in a starting line-up of cars

**radar** a system of high-powered radio waves that shows the position of distant objects

**radiator grille** the metal bars that protect the front of a car radiator (cooling system)

**satellite** a small spacecraft that flies round the Earth, sending and receiving radio signals

**streamlined** describes a vehicle that is shaped so that it cuts through the air with little resistance

**suspension** the system of springs and shock absorbers that connects a vehicle to its wheels

**turret** a compartment carrying a weapon on a tank or armoured vehicle, which can rotate (turn round)

**wind resistance** the force exerted by the wind that slows a car down

**welded** two metals joined together by heating the surfaces of the metals until they melt

# WANT TO KNOW MORE?

Here are some places where you can find out a lot more about cars:

## WEBSITES

**http://auto.howstuffworks.com/car.htm**

**http://www.english-online.at/travel/cars/cars-and-how-they-work.htm**

Two detailed guides to how cars and their engines work.

**http://www.buzzle.com/articles/interesting-car-facts.html**

A mixture of fascinating facts about cars.

## BOOKS

**EDGE: Ultimate 20: Supercars**, Tracey Turner (Franklin Watts, 2014)

**To the Limit: Fantastically Fast Cars**, Jim Pipe (Franklin Watts, 2014)

**Motormania: Racing Cars**, Penny Worms (Franklin Watts, 2010)

**Ultimate Cars (series)**, Rob Scott Colson (Wayland, 2014)

**Top Gear: 100 Maddest Cars**, (BBC Children's Books, 2011)

**Mean Machines: Supercars**, Paul Harrison (Franklin Watts, 2014)

**Mean Machines: Racing Supercars**, Paul Harrison (Franklin Watts, 2014)

**Website disclaimer:**
Note to parents and teachers: Every effort has been made by the Publishers to ensure that these websites are suitable for children, that they are of the highest educational value, and that they contain no inappropriate or offensive material. However, because of the nature of the Internet, it is impossible to guarantee that the contents of these sites will not be altered. We strongly advise that Internet access is supervised by a responsible adult.

# INDEX